PIONEERS OF CANADA

FARM LIFE

MEGAN KOPP

Weigl

Published by Weigl Educational Publishers Limited
6325 10th Street SE
Calgary, Alberta
T2H 2Z9

Website: www.weigl.ca

Library and Archives Canada Cataloguing-in-Publication

Kepp, Megan
     Farm life / Megan Kepp.

(Pioneers of Canada)
Includes index.
ISBN 978-1-77071-679-7 (bound).--ISBN 978-1-77071-683-4 (pbk.)

     1. Farm life--Canada--History--Juvenile literature. 2. Frontier and
pioneer life--Canada--Juvenile literature. I. Title. II. Series: Pioneers of
Canada (Calgary, Alta.)

S522.C3K46 2011   j630.971   C2011-904768-3

Printed in the United States of America in North Mankato, Minnesota
1 2 3 4 5 6 7 8 9 0 15 14 13 12 11

072011
WEP040711

Project Coordinator: Jordan McGill
Design: Terry Paulhus

Photograph Credits
Dreamstime: page 9; Getty Images: pages 1, 3, 5, 6, 8, 10, 13, 14, 16, 17, 18, 20, 21, 22; Glenbow Museum: pages 7, 11, 12,
15, 19.

Every reasonable effort has been made to trace ownership and to obtain permission to reprint copyright material. The
publishers would be pleased to have any errors or omissions brought to their attention so that they may be corrected
in subsequent printings.

We acknowledge the financial support of the Government of Canada through the Canada Book Fund for our
publishing activities.

CONTENTS

INTRODUCTION

Land brought many **settlers** to Canada. People grew plants on the land and made money from selling the **harvest**. Farm life could be difficult. Settlers in the 1800s had to work long, hard hours to have food to eat.

When a farmer and his family first came to their land, it was almost untouched by people. There were trees and fields. If the family was lucky, there was water in a creek. There was no grocery store, no hotel or motel to sleep in until a home was built, and no corrals or barns to hold a cow or horse.

The farmer and his family had to build everything using only the tools they brought and the land. The family needed **shelter**. They also needed to **clear** the land to grow plants in the ground. Most farmers built a temporary home to live in while they cleared the land. **Pioneer** farmers had to make difficult decisions and work hard.

A HOMESTEAD TO FARM

The Canadian government offered free **homestead** land on the prairies in the late 1800s. Many homesteaders came to Canada from Europe. They came to better the life of their families. After a long ocean trip, they would travel by train and horse to find their land.

Farmers were given a quarter section of land (160 acres) for free. A farmer was required to do three things to keep his land. First, he had to build a home on the property. Then, he had to stay on the land for at least three years. Finally, he had to clear from 15 to 50 acres of land each year and plant another 10 to 30 acres of **crops**.

FARMER TOOLS

There were no electricity or gas-powered engines on early farms. Work was done by hand. Saws, wedges, and axes were used to cut trees. These trees were then used to make buildings. Boards were nailed together with hammers. Holes were dug with shovels. Gardens were tended with metal hoes.

The Plow

Breaking through thick soil was difficult for farmers. The walking plow made the job easier. After **hitching** horses or oxen in front, the farmer would walk behind to control the plow. He needed to keep it straight and level. The plow had many different sharp surfaces. These surfaces worked together to cut, lift, and turn over soil.

The Sickle and Scythe

During pioneer times, harvesting was done by hand. If the field was round and uneven, farmers used a short, curved blade called a sickle to cut the stalks of grain or hay. If the field was more open, they could use a long-handled scythe. This tool cut more stalks with one stroke.

Springtime was a busy time for farmers. They would hitch up their horses or oxen and plow the land to get it ready for planting.

M̲ost early pioneer farmers planted crops and raised **livestock**. Cows and pigs were the most common animals raised. Pigs needed little attention, and they would eat almost anything. Cows provided milk. Milk could also be made into butter and cheese.

PLANTING THE CROPS

Many pioneers brought seeds from their homeland to plant their first crop. Walking through the fields, they would plant seeds of wheat, corn, rye, or oats. In the family garden, they planted vegetables and fruit.

VEGETABLE GARDENS

Gardens were an important source of fresh food for farmers. Lettuce, tomatoes, peas, and fruits and berries could be eaten when they were ripe. Other vegetables, such as cabbage, beets, carrots, onions, potatoes, and turnips, were stored for winter months.

IN THE SUMMER

Once the crops were planted, they were left to grow. Vegetable gardens needed regular **weeding** and watering. Days were filled clearing more land. Oxen are strong, and they were often used for this hard work. Trees were cut and stumps and stones removed. New fences were built, and old ones fixed.

Horses were used for riding into town for supplies. They also pulled wagons and plows.

Caring for livestock was a daily chore. Cows needed to be milked. Horses, sheep, and oxen needed to be put out to the pasture. Extra hay and grains were planted during summer to feed the animals once winter came.

CHILDREN ON THE FARM

When they were old enough, girls worked in the vegetable garden and helped feed chickens, gather eggs, and milk cows. They also picked berries and edible plants, cared for younger children, mended clothes, and helped with laundry.

Many children did not go to school if they were needed on the farm. If they did go to school, chores were done in the morning and evening.

Boys were responsible for feeding livestock, hauling water, and gathering firewood. They also helped build and repair fences, hunted and fished for food, and helped clear the land when needed.

During fall, the family prepared for winter. Crops in the fields and fruits and vegetables from the gardens were harvested before the first heavy frost. Grain was stored. Food was preserved so it would not go bad. Firewood was gathered, chopped and stacked for the long winter months ahead. From dawn to dusk, the family was working.

During harvest, everyone worked in the fields to bring in the crop. The crops were cut and tied into bundles. These bundles were propped up together to dry. Once dry, they were stored.

Winter months were spent fixing tools and clothes and making plans for the next growing season. Men fixed farm tools and cleaned guns. Women spun yarn, made candles and soap, and sewed warm quilts and new clothes. Winter was also a good time to visit with family and neighbours.

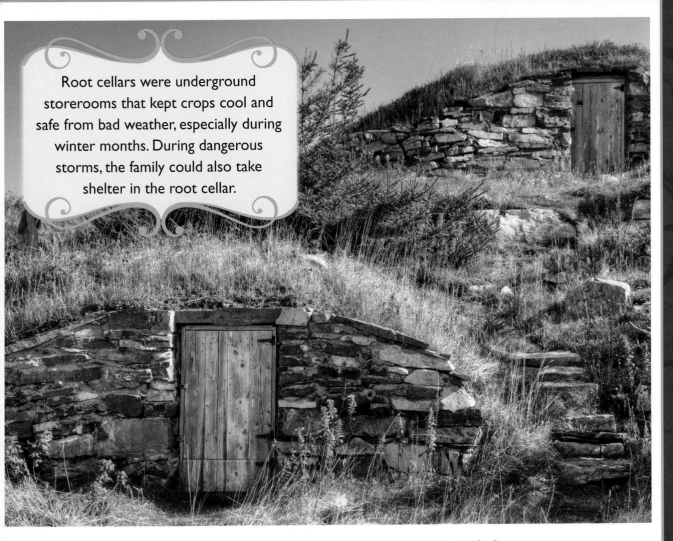

Root cellars were underground storerooms that kept crops cool and safe from bad weather, especially during winter months. During dangerous storms, the family could also take shelter in the root cellar.

Feeding large families took much food. Refrigerators did not exist yet to keep food fresh. Women would hang vegetables such as onions to dry. Hardy vegetables such as carrots and beets were stored in underground root cellars. Other foods would be preserved by pickling, canning, smoking, or salting.

FARMERS TODAY

GRAIN FARMER

Many of today's grain farmers are third-generation farmers. Farms are much larger today. The average farm size in Saskatchewan, a large producer of grain, is 1500 acres. This is almost 10 quarter-sections of land. Today, almost all jobs on the farm are done by large machinery.

Then and Now Diagram

DIAGRAM

Working on a farm in pioneer days was very different from modern times. The diagram on the right compares these differences and similarities. Copy the diagram in your notebook. Try to think of other similarities and differences to add to your diagram.

THEN
- Most families farmed.
- Farmers and their families often made their own clothing, furniture, and tools.
- There were no electric or gas powered engines on farms.
- Farms were only one quarter-section of land.

- Spring is a busy time for farmers because they have to prepare the land for planting.
- Caring for livestock is a daily chore.
- During winter, farmers prepare for winter by harvesting their crops.

NOW
- Few families farm.
- Farmers and their families buy their clothing, furniture, and tools.
- Electricity and gas powered engines are a large part of farms.
- Farms are 10 quarter-sections of land.

GLOSSARY

clear: remove rocks and plants

crops: plants that are grown as food

harvest: to gather plants grown as food

hitching: fastening one object to another

homestead: a parcel of land in the Canadian West granted to a settler by the government

livestock: farm animals kept for a purpose

pioneer: a person who is among the first to settle a new country or area

settlers: people who are among the first to live in a new country or area

shelter: a place that gives protection from weather

weeding: removing unwanted plants from an area

INDEX